AT THE FRONT DOOR OF THE ATLANTIC

para Tony Kerrigan
Picasso

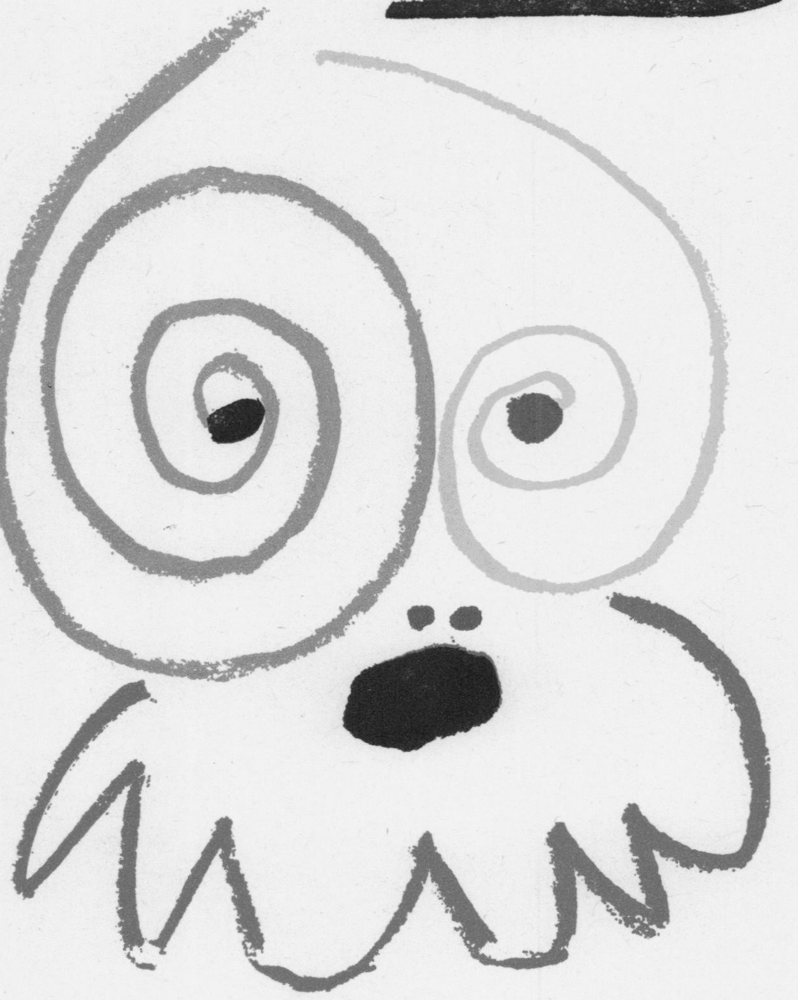

ANTHONY KERRIGAN

At the
Front Door
of the
Atlantic

FRONTISPIECE BY PICASSO

DUBLIN: THE DOLMEN PRESS
CHESTER SPRINGS: DUFOUR EDITIONS

Set in Plantin type with Centaur and Arrighi italic display and printed and published in the Republic of Ireland at The Dolmen Press Limited, 8 Herbert Place, Dublin 2.

*Distributed outside Ireland, except in the U.S.A. and Canada
by Oxford University Press
and in the U.S.A. and Canada by Dufour Editions Inc.,
Chester Spring, Pennsylvania 19425.*

1970

Contents

III *Prayer for Relics*

for Elaine

in France, Spain and Ireland, in those years
and Italy, Portugal, and Switzerland, those months
and even
at the back door of the Atlantic, in the U.S.A.,
those years, too.

Acknowledgements

Most of these poems have appeared in the following magazines: *Álamo* (Salamanca: in Spanish & English), *Arena* (Dublin), *The Atlantic Monthly* (Boston), *Chicago Choice*, *Indice* (Madrid: in Spanish & English), *The Kilkenny Magazine*, *The London Magazine*, *New Mexico Quarterly* (Albuquerque), *New York Times*, *Papeles de Son Armadans* (Madrid/Palma de Mallorca: in Spanish & English), *Poetry* (Chicago), *Poetry Ireland* (Dublin), *Quest* (N.Y.), *Sewanee Review* (Tenn.), *Texas Quarterly* (Austin), *Transatlantic Review* (London-N.Y.), *Voices* (Vinalhaven, Maine). Five of the poems appeared in the collection *Lear in the Tropic of Paris* (Barcelona).

Poetry first printed the following: "Druidical", "Wilderness Bred into a Plant" (printed in Chicago as "Wildness Bred into a Plant"), "Childhood Vision of Virtu", "Canicular Acrostic", "For Two Ladies Ascending a Bus", "The Zion of Echoing Sound".

There were two broadsheet printings of the ballad *Mary Jordan* in previous form, one in an edition of 100 by the Dolmen Press, and the other by St. Sepulchre's Press, handset, with decorations, in an edition of 125 copies.

The drawing by Picasso was made for the author at *La Californie*, Cannes.

I

Distance

Distance

The distance between Cape Cod and Joppa
is terrible—and after all not so great.
Jeremiah Stone:
Journal of an Imaginary Voyage to Zion

There were
        lobster pots
off Scituate bay
that were like jockeys in the line-up.

The sea there
        was a mystery
of families' rights,
of titles to till and terrace the deep.

They fished
        in the wind and brine
as if they had planted orchards
and came to pick the Damson plums.

High on the cliffs
        the apples signalled
the odors of full summer
standing in the cheek of the sea.

The sea weed
        spread to dry
made a frugal pudding
for Yankees who Sundayed

in clapboard churches
                    and sang hymns
as plain as water in the clear air
under belfries with the modest loom of lighthouses.

(Outside the open windows
the windswept gravestones
waved in the tall grass.)

The Books of the Bible
                    and their own names
somehow leagued them
with the farther shore of the Levantine Sea.

Appointment: Just before Noon

AN OBITUARY

Judas rode with Jesus
and Loeb with Leopold
   in the slip of the wind
above the *Seneca* Hotel
where Louis Greenberg never
picked up the phone for fear of foulplay.

Across town, on the *Mark Twain*
the girls shimmied in the wind that tore their posters.

Leaving promptly from La Salle Street
Station, the Eleven-
   Twenty-Two Limited
bit into the grime leading to Cicero
and hurled its gauntlet
   at the flying newspapers.

The marrow of a spoiled Christ worked in his
   every word and deed: what
he shrieked into the other end of the phone
or bellowed at the girls
   as the wind whipped their pants
photographed to mural amplification.

The dum-dum message he took
with no accolade,
   the beer-barrels
of his veins bursting asunder
in the greying street where the grass
was sprinkled with broken glass.

At Dawn

Like a brown tabloid
                the crippled man lay against
the angle of the empty street.
His crutches and the missing leg
                formed a dishevelled swastika
on the wall of the unconscious synagogue.

Why! a fallen man, if he be fallen
from two legs, is a thing of stilled
beauty now, if not long down, and not a clown on stilts,
someone like a lithe skater flung across blue ice
or a dancer at dawn where Carnival jousts with Pentecost:

but shorn of as little as one leg
a man is prisoner to a wet street turning amber.

This man was daubed here, I tell you!
He's a deliberated smear!

Exile

Down the hall the door
closes like corsets close
around a thick-desired
leg and purple-shadowed

thigh in close embrace,
promising far liberty,
as for a Tsar in vast
Russia's inner past.

And that is the dilemma:
whether to force the door
closed in deep embrace
or wait the door's decision,

rap at the parish church
at dawn, drawn and wan
with metaphysic sweat
or gamble on vulgar sleep:

to attack one's nation's odor,
defend its whorish age,
cry treason at self-identity,
succumb to topographic choice.

In the end one burns all night:
the footsteps come and go
and tear one's listening sleep:
police peer through the latch,

a cry torn from memory
apes the bitter concierge.
The police depart, the bread-cart
comes, and death is life.

Abode in Paris

Underground the River Styx
flows in the form of the Métro.
Above, the mirror on the wall reflects
Catulle Mendès in Montparnasse
and a number of run-down family pantheons.

Between heaven and hell they lived, shoplifting eggs:
which shiny and bland informed on their owners.

A hateful redundancy abounded: the eggs, the cemetery
in the mirror, each other's eyes each time they died.

They stole the paper flowers from the foot
of Baudelaire's tomb as only decoration for their room.

Then they left, and fell in love again in Delft.

Cimitière Montparnasse, 1952

Lear in the Tropic of Paris

My love was eaten alive by a street,
consumed in the corner pavilion:
iron knives of the grill-work's attack
covered her sudden lack.

Paris peach in the sky went with her
down the dead end street:
where her eyes hung back from fall's chandelier
Verneuil ran from Saints-Pères.

The Seine washed up its tuberose
in banks with plant's late leaves:
the arrested murmur of the pregnant sound
latticed the square where she drowned.

A vacuum of farewells livened the hour,
silence's grey beaux arts:
I transferred my iris to the yellow flocks
enceinte on a wall by the rocks:

annihilated wall breeding families
pockmarked with rococo bullets:
for a moment the light bloomed like hydrangea
tinting my hands like Lear

alone in the northern tropics, strange
and speckled in the anomalous light.
Had she too found her tropical
palm, some dim vestry's fall?

18

Alone like a salmon recollected the daughters
and their blush but abandonment, night fear:
behind plants, by a palm uncracked in the sunset,
does my love, like a leopard, peer?

Wilderness Bred into a Plant

Man, then, is only man in pain,
and is in pleasure but a flowering sprout,
something piled in proletarian markets,
in single heaps of spice at Marrakesh, or fish in pairs
at Barcelona; a bunch of fragrant watercress.
In pain he falls below a smouldering chestnut,
charred and strong, but clarifies a place,
defines a very Luxembourg; and then at length
becomes a phrase in local awe, a word
he himself will write, a sentiment of horror
he must outlive, and doing so cause wonder.

Heresy in Normandy

For Domrémy-la-Pucelle
and Tom Rowe

Mysticism here gets lost among
the crab apples.
The inland frontier marches like a wood
to the boulder-piled shore
where beaches worthy of Turner's wrecks
coast time's grey indifference.

Out-of-plumb slate belfries
crow like blue cocks in the wet,
blackberries string the graves with lights,
the tides jettison the strand.
Walking the holy lands of nettle-
choked tombs, under the leafy moon,
girls in Normandy breathe heresy
as Paris and London turn with orthodox strife.
Orthodoxy here gets lost among
the crab apples.

S.S. Universe *at Havre*

> "... an audience for whom the world
> was still an object small enough for
> them to cuddle in their hands like
> a bubble-glass of brandy".
>
> Ruthven Todd: *Tracks in the Snow*

What was odd in the port morning
in the frame of the nets and the booms in line
was the cinquepace of dissipated sailors
comrades of the night
                and their red friends.

Bobbing crazily, the boats parodied
the dance, while the epicenes, precisely
the epicenes sang the red songs
rather raggedly, their arms around each other's necks,

blinded by Samson odours and salt cuts.
Salt-lashed coils of rope
smelt like women left behind
in bed before the dawn had finished.

Down the shaft alley of sight
the screw turns the wheels of orphism,
wakes of morning, fasts with shellfish,
consideration of the nature of the cosmic tricolor:

Why the "Universe" is tinier than God!
riding at anchor
            in the dram's spume,
in the bright light of a workman's brandy!

Revolt on the Train to Limbo

I

Is it terrorism, abated, slows the trains?
The vicious flies out of Africa insinuate
their commonness relentlessly on the platform.

An unknown
man doubles the cost of my ticket by his misdirection.
Aboard the train I dare not mouth

the name of God

in my maledictions, complaint: ineffable
it shall be, though the temptation is to harp.
I won't say "God," but "Train" failed me.

II

Jehovah of the Tracks save us from our tickets!
Your hand, Your aesthete's hand, limns the limbs
of the speckled women in their seats like haughty

fighting cocks in pens.
Your touch is seen: though not in those

who permit themselves
opinions on the latest Luck, or in the victims

of homosexual barbers.
We slow past churchyards where dry dead are buried.
At unfrequented crossings ancient women coil red flags
for the train charging the air straight as a bull.
Beyond the windows, reforestation mothers the land:
inside, the passengers who have no destiny in heaven or hell
measure their days in soft drinks and unknown stations.
The whole ride isn't worth a woman's head of hair,

her undressed tresses: and yet, what is Limbo but

a perfect calf,
the hollow of a back demanding a hand's caress?

III

It is noteworthy that no landlocked peasants
ride the cars bound in airconditioned bliss for Limbo.
The sea crashes up against the wheels and no sailor,
either, is to be found seated along this unwinding thread.
The station of destination is encompassed in the train:
There is no station but Limbo, and Train is its Prophet.
The people—no fishermen, or vineyard dressers—sense
that they are taken in by flagmen, barbers, customs runners

and conductors
and of a sudden break out in a chorus of the Word,
the mutilated Word, the broken delirious, sullen name of God,
which must not be used because it's worn

and inaccessible to Limbo.

South of France - North of Spain, April - May 1958

                                 Edward Dahlberg

spoke of the daughters of Lot
                       at Foix:
discovered the Hittite name of Pius IV
                       at Toulouse,
where he denied six Apostles church burial:
invented old generations in the night
                       at Bordeaux:
debated the death of St. Vincent
                       in Teresa's Ávila:
denounced the Moabites outside
                       Unamuno's Salamanca:
warned against the sodomitic Figure of the
                       Right Hand at Dos Aguas'
palace in Valencia.
                       Edward Dahlberg
with whom I'd as lief pray, or wail, or sorrow,
                       in these, or other, cathedral-towns.

The Hill of Tara Recollected at Locarno

For Salvador de Madariaga

Beyond Howth and the Skerries,
that Hill: the green, the wet, the wind, the cows.
Not garrulous, no Crown of Thorns, nor berries,
non-committal, non-Christian, mnemophogus.

Pearly, teethy voices sing green songs of forgetfulness,
of a Queen sitting on a pointed rock like a wind-daft
                                giantess.

Here, now, beyond the medieval casement of the Castello Visconti
the Socratic *sindaco* stares at the Alp—
a Madonna for every rocky periphery—
and listens to the exile who spurned the cup.

A roaring fire in the walk-in grate and all the red camellias
attest to a Platonic aristocracy in exile, abiding unbanishable laws.

Not Under the Geometric Sun
of Muslim North Africa

Warping lends wings
to things
        textures
                otherwise plaque-like:
blank plainsong dirges:
dervishes
        (still demons)
                dead as boards in the sun

outside Sephardic cemeteries,
seas
        entelechies
                of marble boats awash

at Tangier, Xauen, Tetuan
undone
        misspelled
                in their Ladino sentiments.

Across the Herculean Straits
the Fates,
        European,
                are warped and gloriously berserk.

Tangier, 1959

27

The Ebro Front - An Offering:
Twenty Years Later

I found the cave where we crouched that
night: O'Bannion had never come out.
No one had ever had time to look for him.
I had not gone back there before.
Inside, in a niche

                in a side wall far back
there was one shoe

                with a hole through the bottom.
A plate filled with mud, shining

                in the yellow glare of my lamp.
And six spent shells

                in the wet.
Six 45-caliber shells in the mud of the plate.

Back Past Sam Morse* with Miro

For the old rubble rouser

Pictographs carp on rock walls
                    teetering precipitously
to discover only their colour
as they fall through space
                    leaving a wake
of ancient, now cinder, stars
at the crotch of a tomb
                    where a man stands leering
above the spread wands of a moon.
And the moon, run through with a crescent,
                    spouts a pout of him
in aeons, in falls from ledges
and never for no moment
                    as he reels to his knees
is the atmosphere about him absent of him,
the anonymous image of an ancient sure-footed billy-goat will.

*It should be borne in mind that Samuel Finley Morse was a painter who incidentally discovered the sharp thick/thin sounds of rhythmic monotony that sometimes fill the airwaves.

The Artist as Schematized Child

for Camilo

Cubist colours of a plane destined
to crash in the snow, a Chinese line,
schematize the altitude at which consciousness
begins, in the rarified air, to cease existing.

As if a child sat to a plate of magic
mushrooms, and then took up mescal
brush and in off-tint ink sketched
the snowstorm from within the crashing plane.

The youngest draughtsman, like a child pianist,
has the surest stroke, and a genial strain
for filling in the quintessential lines of doom,
sure as single-minded in his lack of room:

high as stratospheric premonition
in his marginal scarce-born no-inhibition.

Belmonte: The Cathedral in the Bullring

1   A cathedral by Gaudí
conscientiously unfinished:
his arms flying-buttresses for vaults
his legs the Parque Güell

2   He traced the lines of the *fin-de-siècle*
and moved like a chandelier
or the beginnings of an earthquake

3   Just as there was nothing
before there was Death
there were no Brave Bulls
before Belmonte killed them

4   An Art Nouveau cathedral
which would fall if it were finished

Mary Jordan

O Mary, Mary Jordan O
the hands of Mary Jordan
their like was never seen below
since the Jewy maid swam Jordan

And still I live in hopes to see
the Holy Ground once more

Hands with tongues and wings
can sing and hope to sing like Mary
Jordan's hands can sing
to start a Jesus-spring like Mary

And still I live in hopes to see
the Holy Ground once more

The clatter bones are puky bones
compared to Mary Jordan's bones
which shimmer in her milky hands
like milkmaid's making-morning hands

And still I live in hopes to see
the Holy Ground once more

When Mary Jordan plays her spoons
her silver spoons from Sligo
plays them on her orange knees
her greenly fingers bridle O

And still I live in hopes to see
the Holy Ground once more

Mary Jordan touches clouds
and makes a cloud devoid of water
cry, a cloud that had no water cry,
O Mary, Jewy Mary's Irish daughter

And still I live in hopes to see
the Holy Ground once more

The bush of Armagh, bush
of Sligo, Mayo's bush,
the bushes burning in the Bible
tindered, tendered, touched and liable

And still I live in hopes to see
the Holy Land once more

Mary Jordan's fountain hands
fingers gushing water
Georgian spigots on her knee
tapping fountain water

And still I live in hopes to see
the Holy Land once more

33

Moses-wands at finger yolks
Moses' wells of finger's mouths
ridden by her finger's droughts
the saddles of her fingers ride

And still I live in hopes to see
                    the Holy Land once more

Her trees of hands bear oranges
her fingers leafy figs
her Mary hands bear infants
to dance to her capering jigs

And still I live in hopes to see
                    the Holy Land once more

Fine Girl You Are!

The Dublin Girls

They waddle like the Liffey gulls
the Dublin women
windblown:
except the countless nurses
walking-white prim-lewd
concupiscent
                    the redheads
quim proud
right perverse

coming diagonally across Saint Stephen's Green
forming a decussated Cross
en route to work in wards
or along the aorta of the Grand Canal
they beat on the blood like
                    a country *bodhrán*

bodhrán: large traditional drum

Bloomsday 1965

Rain in Dublin. Eccles Street condemned.
Rain half turning back.
Out at the Martello Tower
seaview of seagreen ruined by Michael Scott
's snot-white bathroom-of-a-late-tony-Irish house
turned inside out in functioning moderne.
Rain half turned back.
Davy Byrnes put behind Duke Street boards.
Barney Kiernan's pub demolished.
"The gentle rain trying not to fall."

The Ormond Hotel plasticized.
Joyce's birthplace in Brighton Square—
seedy genteel—plaqued by a college in New Jersey.
Rain trying hard to turn back. The city falling.

The Good Life

Not acedia even: listlessness
around the house, top floor over Ely
Place, where George Moore's garden waits
—may, soon, go—behind a nunnery falling away below:
inside the room, fellatio and cunnilinctus to mark
the quiet hour, and Opus 18 quartets to recall the will.
Now, these very days, topless tulips in fresh disarray.

Cunnilinctus, say yes,
sounder than heresy.

Aggressive virgins, nun-baiters in the pubs
stage Easter Risings all day long.
Nothing moves in either place—pub or room—
except in vengeance for some good death.
Schadenfreude on the staircase thoughtfully falling,
and each of us, abandoned in spirit at some
rout in the Dublin Mountains, trudging the empty road back
all night and part of every day thereafter.

Dublin. Spring 1967

On Listening to a Mozart Rondo

O volcano! not beneath it but above
the sunlight sounds, the dark re-echoes No!
rocks pile in hurled anathema, lost snow,
the rock-face splitting, high, bound by *of;*
higher, up among the rotten thunder
the air requires not less but always more art,
Mozart's mastery, one's own "Thou art":
here one hears the rondo and cannot go under.

Summer Arrives

The Dublin girls! The Dublin girls!
wear their new undress
with squeamishness. No garter belt
wilderness here, no *embarras de choix*:
only the wildness of a chance lost glance.

And the whole working city on a round the clock
schedule of breeding the redhaired strain.

Stephen's Green seething with knees
of an afternoon in summer: a Punjab
of undressed jodhpurs and red legged grooms.
(The Nigerian students keeping to Kelly's Corner.)

Out of wide-eyed continence and uncut hair
the evasive look of some stellar unchastity.

I had not thought broken teeth
could compass such suggestive symmetry.

Georgian Fall

Mixed marriage of summer and fall
And all the gray roan of the season:
In the squares fires, over Howth cloud:

In a Sunday's sun we watch the mall
Alight with a Swedenborgian glow:
Mystic vestibule for the Georgian rows.

The park (you said) is mirror clear
Or a grisaille window of spiny glass.
The leaded branches of the copper-beech
(I said) are seams in a fearful sphere.

The finest passage in this Bowery city
(You said) is the fan-light street to the square.
Down the tracery of trees in the fountain's reach
(Where you stood) the light was a labyrinth for Lear.

Under the Statue of Grattan on the Green

In College Green the green
is missed
though on the nether side
of Trinity
the tree that Grattan stares
upon
tops the street like Irish
hair.

There must be something left
that Grattan
dreamed. But not much more
of Ireland
than a tree like Irish hair.

Uprising at Easter
1916-1966

Above Fitzwilliam Square in a dawn white fog
the Dublin sea-gulls whirl for Easter,
the surgeons' Jaguars gone out West
for family conclave, leaving city sod

and hydrangeas for the Easter Rising, the lilies
of rebellion. In the Hugeunot Cemetery buds
off Stephen's Green suffer sparrows,
and mockery from Parnell's heirs is near adulterous.

In the dark centre of the city dank,
waste-heaps of a race's ancestors,
settlers in a nowhere of rhetoric, in a West
of sunset, listen on Sony transistors.

The words mean nothing, only the accents
convey a time and place, a total
from the first betrayal. " 'My friends, there are
no friends'. There was no betrayal".

II
The Zion of Echoing Sound

The Trip

To walk as far as she is—
farther than the legend of my father—
is to skirt, carefully lifting the wet branches,
around a blueberry patch.

Horses are yoked to bears
                    in these fields.

One eye is a blue forest, the other the sea.
Bees come to comb their tresses in the apples of her hair.

From time to time, the thought of the sea-splashed granite.

And then, suddenly:
"Here it is!" resounding in the evening snow of the next season,
                                                    at dusk.
And children's voices carrying across the valley like winged icicles.

To go to her is to step
(skirting the wet branches)
                    slowly
over a blueberry patch.

The Zion of Echoing Sound

Looking back these ten years of our love
it is a kind of Schumann music I recall
as the young piano student and I looked out
the windows of the Paris *Conservatoire* at our first fall
chestnut trees seen at the height of the dove.

I looked at the green through the branch of her hair.
The clavier fingers held the Mansard sill.
The Paris sky was the way it always would bear
blue stormy gold. And our look is there still,
gazing out from the echoing sound, by the stair

leading down and out to the Rue de Madrid
and the bridge at the Place de l'Europe, an iron
rainbow of steam from the locomotives below,
a passage into a De Chirico Zion
where our history is and our young age hid.

My Love

I

You are correct, circumspect in size
like the Isabella Stewart Gardner Museum
                       in Boston.
Filled with significant riches
                 like the Frick,
not blown or overborne
             like the Metropolitan.

II

My *pala d'oro* is not the prized one in Venice,
not an altarscreen in pieces-of-eight for a basilica,
no gilt horizon for a procession of blue saints
(treading topaz and amethyst abstractions),
but this girl's lucid flank glancing the sun
off her opaque verticality before she reaches Salute,
Santa Maria's roundhouse terminal of early morning light.

My Jerusalem

A phalanx of Papal feetwashers
    would not suffice to lave
with love your feet enough.

No count of Jesus foot-kisses
    nor spittlefields of Magdalens
would reach beyond your middle calf.

And where you stand your God begins
    the circle of sun and myth:
green and purple, the wound of choice.

The Elders in their bush of beards
    must hide their high obeissance
to see you bathed a full Messiah.

And not by hand is your Temple
    made but joined of fire and myrrh
to house the desert's water.

Canicular Acrostic

tomando en la boca un poco de zumo de orozuz
—old antidote for August

Earth lends us the full crop of her:
Long we hope to harvest there and pasture sure:
Apple-time is in her hair, and the ground around her
Ingle coloured in its fire-wet litter:
Neat-wine breath where locusts stir
Entailed green legs as sweet as her.

"In Virgo's sign are music's spendthrifts"
Naves of eyes, lengths swept with swifts.

Aromatic in the slips of her sandals, she walks like a spice
    tree stinging:
Unorthodox signs in her eyes, her hands are plainsong singing:
Godsends her knees, her armpits a patois of spices:
Upas trees blanch, and bleed their poison as she passes:
She flares in a religion of bushes, flaming in Moses colours:
The tip of her tongue is an herbal, her mouth an orbit of birds.

Expressionist Portrait

There are 230 kinds
of symmetry in space
and 17 kinds of symmetry
on a plane.
Art Manual

On a deserted street corner
                in the suburbs
in the passive winter light, your face
like Siva or the myth of procreation
is the sudden avatar of a morning in childhood.

This powder, the odor of grenadine, this pongee
envelop the translation symmetry of a body,
a porcelain rococo and circuitous sentence
expatiated upon by these glossed limbs.

You are a Havana brought north
the fluid symmetry of a new Hundred Days:
on the plane of you
                are a myriad winter mirrors,
in the space of you

           the odors-to-come are born.

Childhood Vision of Virtu

Bethesda to me
    was our Spanish serving girl
    in high heels for her lover
    her legs untouching the floor
    as they hung over the side of the bed

And I confess
    the Salomonic columns
    of flesh, spiralling in slack
    and tension, the equivocacy of shoes,
    the approach and water of tremor

Influenced me
    in the high religion of fossils
    in rock, the mystic birth
    of working horses' flanks
    from women's holy girth

For I was then
    Susanna's pubic clown
    the elder in me waiting
    with no ulterior intention:
    only the interminable meaning.

110344

¿does verse-gross prose versify?

as on

The Fourth of July:

It was the Fourth of July
on the eve of the field of fireworks
and my cousin said to me
instead of the fireworks
I'll take off my clothes in the attic
if you really want to see
instead of the fireworks
the all and very me

I looked at eve on the field of fireworks
watched from the yard
and did not walk to the field
but watched for a while
the fireworks: the rockets speeding up the sky
the flashes treading the dark and
the pinwheels whirring
but didn't walk out to the field

Watched the fire and flash overhead
and thought of the fire and flash
over my head and the peril and flash
overhead, the nudity over
my young-years-old head, and leaving
the field and the sky to its fireworks rushed
up to the attic above
where
my cousin was already more than naked.

For Two Ladies Ascending a Bus

Stone stables without horses in winter
are not more bleak in abandon
than this mauve touring coach
without these ladies ascending.
They run flanks not seen outside a hippodrome,
pull taut the earth to the runner,
decorate the home stretch with tense leather.

Shaking the tall tops of the forests in their thighs
they still stoop to plant pansies in their clearings.

There is wind on the thick of my watching,
wind on the thighs of my choice.

Among all the other births in their livelong day
they give birth to the space taken up by this mooncalf bus.

Two Figures

The consequential melon lips
              of the Negress
on the stork's legs
speak of anti-platinum,
of lemon tones in her companion.

Unlike the porcelain Negress
              in the Metropolitan
she does not "show Time in her eyes"
but rather stands to illustrate
the immediate sense of bliss

more or less historyless,
              and yet a page
or book illuminated with a mum
processional and she the churchman

to the procession of her companion.
              The two
made love of colour, coloured
the sound of the summer day,
and drew quick sketches across the sun.

When one moved or fended
              the other dawned,
the light of one shivered lightly
in the evening of the other's moon:
unlike lilies they toiled and spun.

Fluid Woman

Through long use the melancholy in her eyes
has now become adverbial.
Her irises are nests of participles,
her substantives need never jell.

Her hair corroborates the black equivocation
in her eyes; the foreign roots
of her nouns are verbs in fission,
her teeth are paraphrase to lily shoots.

There is no no-man's land about her:
the trenches face each other
and both by grammarians were
held in turn before by her.

Eurasian Girl

There is no polemic between East and West
in that moving jet ivory face, no
cloud over the still spring, nor darkest
current in the set of cross-cut agate.
She walks as wisely as the mandarins go

and in her hair the shadows in Saskia's dark hair
where her husband made brown into colour of infinity.
Standing clear, where she is dark she is also fair
against the horizon of her lithe history.
Small wonder her eyes mirror the Amsterdam sky.

She holds her veil of hair across
her mouth to muse: if Vermeer had seen
her dulcet distant listening to the loss
of sound as a horse draws the scene
of morning landscape after him in the blue scheme

of Sunday morning, with oranges and kitten,
he might have painted her gold-flecked
in bed, dark and fair amid the heavy linen
watching, with the air of hearing Mass,
her Sunday watcher and acolyte, her *djin-djin*.

Miriam

it's not all washed-out blue eyes you are
under the supermarket neon—
corpse not yet undressed for the slab—
even morgue marble has veins:

a right keening sound off you drowns
out the supermarket-music, the white
marble to lay you on is seen to vein,
a blush begins to spread, you're not dead

and in the encounter, neither am I

To the Fan-Fall *said the Sign*

To the Fan-Fall! To the Fan-Fall!
we rushed, crushing the hedges of ferns and the fuchsias,
running half-naked in the filtered sunlight and dark in the shade,
and crashed through the thickets on to the carpet
of small green, and then, coming and going in the thrashing grass,
in her arms, in her hair, in her caracol ear
still crying: *To the Fan-Fall! To the Fan-Fall!*

III

Prayer for Relics

In the Mouths of the Weeds and the Cheeks of their Horses

What grass awaits us
and undisclosed winds?
Who walks above
not yet met?

The feet we must know
are by now known,
though we may never move
to kiss or caress them.

Hanging from dissolute mounts
that carelessly wander our graves
the women we never admonished
with love may weigh down our names

where the letters wave in the wind
that sings the chorus of slate,
and we greenly rot in the cheeks
of their horses and the mouths of the weeds.

A Heretical Wind in the Hair

How many strands. . .?
We stand by the sea counting the cleft faces of the wind.
Sand spit and long strand dividing the combers.
Salt spray forked,

repetitive.

The Higher Mathematics of hair
proves:
Heresy. But undermining nothing: sound:
as clear as many-branched seaweed in a blue
sea shifting to clear green. A frontier.

"To have a great Orthodoxy we must have a great Heterodoxy."

O solipsisticism!

And the hair of our head outlives the place of our grace.

And heaven's manes, too, are uncoiled.

for Keith Botsford
hombre completo,
and Zhiva

Corrida

The bull with the glass horns
weaves his garlanded afternoon
spewing virgins and stocks.

The bull with the glass horns
rounds the fearful sphere
of Pascal with awful paradox.

Bull, charge and toss up the sea!

The man with gangrene in his sword
works his golden wounds
lolling his head for impetus.

Bull, charge and toss up the sky!

The bull with the glass horns
would marry the man with the gangrene
deceive him on his death bed.

The man with gangrene in his sword
is married to the bull with horns
and waits upon his deathbed.

Bull, charge and toss up your lover!

Will in the Bullrushes

Where on the river is sweet sleep swept?
Where does one's Moses go?

Swart glaze of water, a whore's thin eyes:
where eddies won't swim, don't trust in the water.

Roe-speckled rushes close on the sound
as boy's little barkentine boats.

Salivating blackamoors, caskets
set out on the tide: these moon's sole dominoes

appear in the offshore, waiting for rain:
the ghost-ship shudders, her palms' timbers strain:

Float will wild, all of your will float wild,
still source of water won't stop in its flow:

ritual of relics by water, polish of bones aesthetic:
the polished will well no matter is one's sole relic.

Prayer for Relics

That wall wills windows
against which rains would shower
                             and roses blow:
throw the eager stone!

Those windows want walls
                          though not all
the roses turn into cloisters
to house the zealous bone.

Shooting Rockets to the Virgin

Where the dimples of gunpowder
rock in the sky
the eyes of believers
turn blue with surprise:

O see the ascent, the wane,
the wave out at sea:
will she rock on the water
or billow the rain?

The small far-off
cannon surrounding
the hills redound
round the altar

in a murmur of gladioli shoots
tendered by women,
to the cannons of candles'
purblind delight.

Where one watches hermetically the heart
unseals: Send now
my segment of sea
some portion of the fields'

blue cabbage,
gunpowder love
for her veins of blue
and the enormous idea of her white.

An Ex-Voto *in an old* Roman *Town*

SANTIAGO DE ALCUDIA

I

Gold collage of
beneficiary's eyes

hang by hanging
Christ and wear

a gold cast
that passes peace

and under their yellow
ribbon search

a hyperopic heaven.

II

Gold pupils
wafer thin

dance their con-
secration, iris

moons wavering
across the waters

of Christ's wood:
horses of grapes

treading sack.

This good Virgin, then

This good virgin, then, hung in the brothel:
done by Crivelli, originally:
the fruit on the tapestry at the side of the figure
(which served by way of Italian delight)
bringing a superlative notion of nature into the room.

Outside, in the sun now, the cabbages,
blue upon blue row, demonstrated
the local peasant frugality, and more,
the intensity of the sensual use of the soil,
especially where its face was kissed into roses.

So that the man on the bed un-alone
was humbly delighted and breathed thanks
that the Italian had gotten himself up on the wall
and the peasants had kissed the soil into passion
sometime before he chanced upon the sensual conception.

The Vertical Player

for Carmen and Irving Feldman

The vertical man, like a thief,
connects with God, the god

of his fathers or with others invented
on the spur of the moment by composers,

pianists unknown or unplaying:
the concourse always in earnest, serious

in their shyness as they smile to the music,
in love with their viols, their fingers.

And he is his church, gothic his humour,
and a fourth man to the three

other players. The trio augmented,
the Trinity with him plays quartets

where he steps up to them
assuming his place with affection

for his fellows Who in sum are more
than his one man's

instrumentation and compass
but like him are always in love.

Eleven as Epiphany

Twelfth Night is for aliens
                to Ireland.
The eleventh, in odd uniqueness is my undoing.

Lazarus knows my meaning, his mouth
A sink of garlic on the far aïolli shore.

Sheamus and Red O'Duggan and Levy
Those were the boys that gathered close and traipsed

Around the Maypole of Our Lord
Their eyes bandconcerts of waltzes in the hush of the green.

The Jew showed himself more naked
                than May
On the Twelfthtide of the Twelfthday.

The Eve and not the End is sacred:
Though the Hebrews had no iron hieroglyphics

For any number even ten
                or twelve,
The Eleventh Night is virgin to the Twelfth.

The Wall

The mind is dying! Long live the body!
was written on a wall in an anguish of windows;
and underneath and to one side was chalked in white
A bas les mulâtres!
                   an order on the coloured man. (Or the white?)

And when, now, is a mulatto coloured, and when
                                is he white?
Or does it depend on the state, in which state the union?
The mind is less than one thirty-second of the body,
less than the coloured blood in that mulatto there.

The mind is mulatto to the body, a miscegenation,
a wilful abdication to a wall anguishing windows.

Waters of Melis*

for Carles Riba, Catalan classicist

Waters of wood, waters of waters
verse couched like veins in the Pyrenees marble at Vich
or the leprous spots on the Romanesque Lazarus at Tahull

wood-knots and nodes of stone rhetoric
mellifluous grain and fiber of a fading dogma
decipherable as flights of birds in the iris of a heretic

On one noon-bell day, the light a stigma
and the cypress silhouetted red against the tympanum
of sky, we strolled the length of separate enigma

speaking of the texture of turgid signs in gum,
he of waters of wood, mute dactylology of God,
I of waters of waters, grain and vein of oblivion.

*Melis: *Catalan word for a certain variety of pine and its wood, used in cabinet-making.*

One day, Charles Riba said to me: "I was just admiring the wood panelling in my room: I saw such graceful patterns there, such beautiful waters of melis".

Orestes in Excelsis

Circumcision is nothing,
uncircumcision is nothing ...
(I Cor., 7, 19)

He had written his *Liber Chaos*
penned his bloody page
of penmanship:
and not a word had passed into Law.

Thus disinherited, the eyes,
of that disinterested blue
the English call grey,
were further refined by the side of the wine-dark sea.

Proto-godfather to a god
he would not succumb
to the fennel leaves of his knees
as he stood in the dry wheat wind.

St. Jude the Obscure,
St. Thursday, St. Ezra
of the Head, St. Dymphna
pray for him and keep him!

The Ethic Egg

A gloss on José Luis Aranguren

Rectitude,
like an eggshell,
is close covering for the trajectory
of a body

the anti-elliptic
projection, the helical
flowering and fall
of a being.

Rectitude
is not a balance
nor an undiscovered hemisphere
but the look

shut against
the yellow tongues
of bursting myrtles swarming
in a void.

Rectitude
released is a giant
roc egg too huge to have
been broken.

Brief Lament for Almighty God

"... the conjecture that the
Almighty is also in search
of Someone, and *that* Someone
in search of some superior
Someone (or merely indispensable
or equal Someone) and thus on
to the end—or better, the
endlessness—of Time".

Jorge Luis Borges: *Ficciones*

The least mans' heart breaks for the Almighty searching out His peer,
The indispensable, merely equal Power which would make palpable
the idea of God to Him,
His shadow, contour, jaw casting an outline upon the staggering
mists.

What worth the bed, fault, stratum harbouring the sand dollar of His
imprint?
What fossil of the Holy Ghost in the form of miraculous fish will
satisfy
That parthenogenetic multiplying need to conjugate the aorist tense
of a past moment without continuity?

The repetitiveness of God is His only surety: for the deaths of men
Console but do not assuage. The pure, the least man will not require
The death of God, His annihilation, where He strives to find His
image.
We do not need God's shadow, jaw, His contour. Lord of Hosts, He
does.

75

The Saints' Relics, then,

The saints' relics, then, in all the Gothic
vaults, the ex-votos in silver, the simple-minded
or complex gravestones and pantheons are all proven
folly? The word Zeus—the concept as well as the man,
the naked God, frolicking or grim—is obsolescent?

And the dismal spaces have invaded the day:
and the labyrinth is pressed flat, the way
through made straight, the boxwood cut
and the hedges, behind which daft dalliance
engendered prodigies to make men rival roses,
have given way to non-stop throughways.

So be it: let the polishing of metal hoods replace
stone phalluses or Communion with thirteen Jews,
and whatever schism threaten matter break our space.

Over Es Colomer

for John and Jean Barnes

Wind, the crayfish, a phallic plant:
that was the afternoon's triangulation.
Beyond it as background a horizon
beginning, in the centre, to decussate.

The crayfish and the phallic plant
formed a working pair,
                    and the wind,
the wind stirred the roots of line
on the horizon where it strove to filament.

If the afternoon had come apart from fault
it would have raveled into wild artichoke hearts,
asparagus spears, phallic crayfish, and wind
laying low the green reedy grass with salt.

Druidical

Fell death
deliver me
from the verses in your eyes

Old oblivion
succour me
from any more surprise.

Obvious tomb
cover me
from insidious clothes

With a blank inscription
hide me
from the closest prose.

From involute prayer
spare me
or un-Latin mass

Immured in simplicity
buttress me
with windblown grass.